The Culinary
Art of Fika

A Scandinavian Food Odyssey
Featuring 30 Recipes

Emma Alice Nilsson

Table of Contents

Introduction

One of the most famous Scandinavian pleasures is getting together for coffee and something sweet, and here in Sweden we do it frequently. It enables us to sit, interact with others, and engage in casual conversation.

Recently, there has been a rising prevalence of eating Nordic baked goods. This is primarily due to the growing practice of Fika and that Swedish food is mainly composed of berries and stone fruits, crisp and soft (often sugared) loaves of bread, and cultured dairy products.

Many different types of bread, including flatbreads and crispbreads, are used in Swedish cuisine. You can produce these loaves of bread from rye, wheat, oat, sourdough, or whole grains. Numerous sweetened bread varieties exist, some of which contain spices.

The primary fat sources are butter and margarine, while olive oil is gaining popularity. Various yeast buns, cookies, biscuits, and cakes are part of Sweden's pastry culture; many are pretty sweet and frequently served with coffee (Fika). Nordic cuisine is straightforward and healthy, made with the land's staple products.

We have a wide variety of delectable, easy-to-make cakes and other delectable morsels because we adore Fika. These tasty treats fit nicely on the kitchen table and are ready to cut, share, or grab as you please.

30 Simple Scandinavian Recipes

Molasses Cookies

Molasses cookies are thin, highly crumbly cookies or biscuits. These are frequently linked to the long Christmas season. Molasses cookies are traditionally thinner than typical cookies and are covered with glaze and candy.

These cookies are frequently used as window decorations in Norway and Sweden. Many families have a history of baking Molasses cookies with their children.

Preparation Time: 20 Minutes
Cooking Time: 20 Minutes
Serves: 4

Ingredients

- Demerara Sugar, 128g (4.5 oz)
- Kosher Salt, 2.8g (0.9 oz)
- Molasses, 16.7g (0.66 oz)
- Two Large Eggs
- Ground Allspice, 14.3g (0.5 oz)
- Ground Ginger, 5.7g (0.16 oz)
- Salted Butter, 128g (4.5 oz)
- White Sugar, 64g (2.25 oz)
- Flour, 448g (15.8 oz)
- Vanilla Extract, 5.7g (0.16 oz)

Instructions

1. Take out a large bowl
2. Add the dry ingredients into the bowl
3. Mix all the dry ingredients well
4. Add the butter into the wet mixture
5. Add the eggs into the mixture
6. Add the demerara sugar, molasses and allspice
7. Make small round cookies and place them on a baking dish
8. Bake at 350°F/177°C for 20 minutes
9. Serve once cooled down

Pumpkin Cake

Try this straightforward recipe for pumpkin cake for those who want pure pumpkin and spice flavors without any additional flavorings. A prominent taste and an incredibly moist texture are promised by using brown sugar and one cup of pumpkin puree.

Even while it's fantastic on its own, you'll adore this cake with a piping hot cup of coffee, or perhaps tea, if that's what you fancy!

Preparation Time: 10 Minutes
Cooking Time: 20 Minutes
Serves: 4

Ingredients

- Kosher Salt, 2.84g (0.1 oz)
- Sugar, 128g (0.8 oz)
- Ground Nutmeg, 2.84g (0.1 oz)
- Pumpkin Puree, 128g (4.5 oz)
- Ground Cinnamon, 5.7g (0.16 oz)
- Freshly Ground Cardamom, 8.4g (0.33 oz)
- Unbleached White Flour, 256g (9.0 oz)
- Unsalted Melted Butter, 128g (0.8 oz)
- Baking Soda, 5.7g (0.16 oz)
- Use Three Eggs

Instructions

1. In a bowl, add your three eggs
2. Beat eggs until they become frothy and creamy
3. Add the melted butter into the mixture
4. Add the sugar and continue beating the mixture for five more minutes
5. Fold the pumpkin puree into the wet mixture
6. In a separate bowl, add all the dry ingredients
7. Slowly add your wet mixture into your dry mixture and fold your batter
8. Pour your mix into a greased baking dish
9. Bake for 15-20 minutes at 350°F/177°C
10. Serve once cooled down

Pineapple Tart

As with other traditional foods like American apple pies and Swedish meatballs, everyone's an expert when it comes to making pineapple tarts, and we all have our preferred method that is, by definition, the best. However, you cannot choose your favorite flavor, size, crust, or color of jam, with or without "crown," etc., until you have tried them all.

I enjoy it with jam placed on a pastry foundation with a light golden brown color that turns out to be crisp and caramelized on the surface and moist on the inside.

Preparation Time: 10 Minutes
Cooking Time: 30 Minutes
Serves: 4

Ingredients

- Butter, for greasing
- Pineapple Chunks, 64g (2.25 oz)
- Eggs, One
- Sugar, 64g (2.25 oz)
- Cream, 64g (2.25 oz)
- Tart Dough, as required
- Butter, 64g (2.25 oz)
- Golden Syrup, 28.3g (1 oz)

Instructions

1. In a large bowl, add cream and beat it thoroughly
2. Make the cream frothy and add the sugar
3. Remix the mixture and add the butter

4. Continue beating the mixture and add the golden syrup, egg, and pineapple chunks
5. Lay the tart dough into greased tart dishes
6. Add the pineapple mixture on top of the tarts
7. Bake your mix for 20-30 minutes at 350°F/177°C
8. Let the pastries cool down and serve

Brown Bread

Brown bread is made mainly from whole grains, wheat, and occasionally from dark-colored additives like molasses or coffee. It is whole wheat bread in Canada, Ireland, and South Africa, but molasses-made bread is typical in the Maritimes and New England. In some places in the US, brown bread is called wheat bread to complement white bread.

Preparation Time: 10 Minutes
Cooking Time: 20 Minutes
Serves: 4

Ingredients

- Unsalted butter for greasing
- Baking Molasses, 64g (2.25 oz)
- Brown Sugar, 128g (4.5 oz)
- Buttermilk, 256g (9.0 oz)
- Baking Soda, 5.7g (0.16 oz)
- All-Purpose Flour, 192g (6.7 oz)
- Golden Syrup, 128g (4.5 oz)
- Baking Powder, 16.7g (0.5 oz)

- Whole Wheat Flour, 384g (13.5 oz)
- Two Eggs

Instructions

1. In a large bowl, add the eggs
2. Beat eggs until they become frothy and creamy
3. Add the melted butter and golden syrup into the mixture
4. Add brown sugar and beat the mixture for five more minutes
5. In another bowl, add the dry ingredients
6. Gingerly add your dry mixture into the wet mixture
7. Next, fold your batter
8. Bake your bread for 15-20 minutes at 400°F/200°C
9. Add the bread to a rack when finished baking
10. Let the bread cool down, then proceed to slice and serve

Sour Cream Twist

Despite having yeast, these cookies resemble pastries and do not rise. One of the best Swedish Christmas customs only requires chilling the dough for a bit, rolling in plenty of sugar, and twisting. We produce these each year. I enjoy dipping them in hot cocoa!

Preparation Time: 20 Minutes
Cooking Time: 20 Minutes
Serves: 4

Ingredients

- Kosher Salt, 2.84g (0.10 oz)
- White Sugar, 64g (2.25 oz) for spreading on top
- Large Eggs, Use Two
- Yeast, 14.3g (0.50 oz)
- Salted Butter, 128g (4.5 oz)
- White Sugar, 64g (2.25 oz)
- Full-Fat Sour Cream, 128g (4.5 oz)
- Flour, 448g (15.8 oz)
- Vanilla Extract, 5.7g (0.16 oz)

Instructions

1. Take out a large bowl
2. Add the dry ingredients into the bowl
3. Mix the ingredients well
4. Add the white sugar and yeast into a bowl with two tablespoons of hot water 9.8ml (0.33 oz)
5. Place the yeast mixture in a damp/moist area
6. In a separate bowl, mix the full-fat sour cream and salted butter
7. Beat your cream and butter to form a homogenized mixture
8. Add the butter mixture to your wet ingredients
9. Add the yeast mixture and eggs into your dough mixture
10. Add the formed mixture into a piping bag
11. Next, make a twist in the dough on the baking tray
12. Add some white sugar on top of your twists and bake for 15-20 minutes at 350°F/177°C
13. Let your biscuits cool down before serving

Cardamom Tea Loaf

Quick bread, often known as tea cakes or tea loaves, has long been among my favorite things to bake. They're simple to make and excellent for eating. Since cardamom is one of my favorite spices, I used it organically in this dish. Although not quite as dense, it has pound cake-like characteristics.

Preparation Time: 10 Minutes
Cooking Time: 20 Minutes
Serves:4

Ingredients

- Kosher Salt, 2.84g (0.10 oz)
- Sugar, 16.7g (0.66 oz)
- Ground Cinnamon, 5.7g (0.16 oz)
- Freshly Ground Cardamom, 8.4g (0.33 oz)
- Sour Cream, 128g (4.5 oz)
- Eggs, Three
- Unbleached White Flour, 256g (9.0 oz)
- Unsalted Melted Butter, 128g (4.5 oz)
- Baking Soda, 5.7g (0.16 oz)

Instructions

1. In a large bowl, add your eggs
2. Beat the eggs until they turn frothy and creamy
3. Add the sour cream and melted butter into your mixture
4. Add the sugar and beat the mixture for five more minutes
5. In a separate bowl, add all the dry ingredients

6. Slowly add your wet mixture into your dry mixture and fold your batter
7. Pour your mixture into a greased baking dish
8. Bake your loaf for 15-20 minutes at 350°F/180°C
9. Let the tea loaf cool down and serve

Apple Cake With Vanilla Sauce

The dessert, Swedish apple cake, is unusual.

You'd be excused for supposing that the apple cake, also known as sockerkaka med äpple (sponge cake with apples) or simply äppelkaka (apple cake), may resemble any other apple cake recipes popular in Europe. However, Swedish apple cake is slightly different; it's a cake/pie hybrid.

Preparation Time: 30 Minutes
Cooking Time: 25 Minutes
Serves: 4

Ingredients

- One, Egg
- Baking Soda, a pinch
- Flour, 128g (4.5 oz)
- Ground Cardamom, 1.42g (0.05 oz)
- Sugar, 16.7g (0.66 oz)

- Butter, 64g (2.25 oz)
- Vanilla Sauce, 128g (4.5 oz)

For The Filling

- Cinnamon, 1.42g (0.05 oz)
- Nutmeg, a pinch
- Butter, 64g (2.25 oz)
- Flour, 64g (2.25 oz)
- Sugar, 64g (2.25 oz)
- Blanched Almonds, 64g (2.25 oz)
- Apples, 128g (4.5 oz)

Instructions

1. Incorporate the dry ingredients in a large bowl to make the cake batter
2. Make the batter and pour it into a baking dish
3. Ensure that the baking dish is greased correctly and lined with parchment paper
4. Cook your apple mixture by mixing up all your ingredients
5. Add your apple mixture into your cake mixture, and do not mix
6. Bake your cake for 20-25 minutes at 180°C/350°F
7. When cooked, let cool down and serve

Walnut Butter Cookies

Shortbread-like Swedish Walnut Butter Cookies are a straightforward dessert. They have a buttery, nutty flavor and a light texture thanks to the addition of powdered sugar to the dough. These delicious treats will be impossible for you to refuse.

Preparation Time: 20 Minutes
Cooking Time: 20 Minutes
Serves: 4

Ingredients

- Kosher Salt, 2.84g (0.10 oz)
- Large Eggs, Use Two
- Yeast, 14.3g (0.50 oz)
- Salted Butter, 128g (4.5 oz)
- White Sugar, 64g (2.25 oz)
- Flour, 448g (15.8 oz)
- Vanilla Extract, 5.7g (0.16 oz)

Instruction

1. Take out a large bowl
2. Add the dry ingredients
3. Combine all the ingredients well
4. Add the Sugar and yeast to a bowl with two tablespoons, 9.8ml (0.33 oz) of hot water
5. Place your yeast mixture in a damp place
6. Add the butter to the wet ingredients
7. Add the yeast mixture and eggs into the cookie mixture
8. Add the formed mixture into a piping bag
9. Pipe small round cookies on a baking dish and bake your cookies at 375°F/190°C for 15-20 minutes
10. Take your cookies out, let them cool down, and serve

Vanilla Bread

A buttery, rich, moist loaf made with the best vanilla bread recipe. This is a straightforward and easy recipe to make a typical handmade vanilla loaf cake that is soft, rich, and delicious. This moist vanilla bread is delectable and has a fantastic flavor.

Below is a simple recipe for one of my all-time favorite cakes. It's a pretty tasty and flavorful vanilla dessert. It has a somewhat fluffier texture than a typical Vanilla loaf and is lovely and moist with a delicious golden top.

Preparation Time: 10 Minutes
Cooking Time: 20 Minutes
Serves: 4

Ingredients

- Kosher Salt, 2.84g (0.10 oz)
- Sugar, 16.7g (0.66 oz)
- Vanilla Essence, 5.7g (0.10 oz)
- Eggs, Use Three
- Unbleached White Flour, 256g (9.0 oz)
- Unsalted Melted Butter, 128g (4.5 oz)
- Baking Soda, 5.7g (0.16 oz)

Instructions

1. In a large bowl, add the eggs
2. Beat the eggs until they turn frothy and creamy
3. Add the melted butter into the mixture
4. Add the sugar and beat the mixture for five more minutes

5. In another bowl, add the dry ingredients
6. Gently incorporate your wet mix into the dry mix and fold your batter
7. Bake your bread for 25-20 minutes at 350°F/180°C
8. Take your vanilla loaf out to cool down; serve when ready

Coffee Bread

Who first created coffee bread is unknown. The delectable dessert seems to have developed from other sweet delicacies. The first coffee bread most likely came from Dresden in Germany. However, coffee bread developed from a variety of ethnic traditions, with the Danish inventing the first instance of eating a form of sweet bread with coffee.

Preparation Time: 10 Minutes
Cooking Time: 20 Minutes
Serves: 4

Ingredients

- Kosher Salt, 2.84g (0.10 oz)
- Sugar, 16.7g (0.66 oz)
- Vanilla Essence, 5.7g (0.16 oz)
- Coffee Grains, blended until fine, 28.3g (1 oz)
- Eggs, Use Three
- Unbleached White Flour, 256g (9.0 oz)

- Unsalted Melted Butter, 128g (4.5 oz)
- Baking Soda, 8.4g (0.33 oz)

Instructions

1. In a large bowl, add the eggs
2. Beat eggs until they become frothy and creamy
3. Add the melted butter and coffee powder into the mixture
4. Add the sugar and beat the mixture for five more minutes
5. In another bowl, add the dry ingredients
6. Slowly add your wet mix into your dried mix and fold your batter
7. Bake your bread for 15-20 minutes at 350°F/175°C
8. Take your coffee bread out and let it cool off; serve when ready

Almond Tart

Served with a cup of espresso, set your Swedish almond tart on a cooling rack.

A "spin-off" of the Swedish Almond Cake is the Swedish Almond Tart (Toscabit). Although both employ almond paste, the primary distinction is that the bottom is covered in pastry dough because this is a tart.

My favorite is when they combine the sliced almonds with caramelized sugar and then drizzle more glaze on top. I've also seen versions where they just sprinkle crushed nuts on top.

Preparation Time: 10 Minutes
Cooking Time: 30 Minutes
Serves: 4

Ingredients

- Butter, for greasing
- Sliced Almonds, 64g (2.25 oz)
- Sugar, 64g (2.25 oz)
- Almond Paste, 28.3g (1 oz)
- Cream, 64g (2.25 oz)
- Tart Dough, as required
- Butter, 64g (2.25 oz)
- Golden Syrup, 28.3g (1 oz)

Instructions

1. In a large bowl, add your cream and beat until it is creamy and frothy, then add your sugar
2. Continue beating the mixture and add the butter
3. Continue beating the mixture adding the almond paste, golden syrup, and sliced almonds
4. Continue mixing thoroughly until all the ingredients are combined properly
5. Lay the tart dough into greased tart dishes
6. Add the almond mixture on top
7. Bake your plate for 20-30 minutes at 375°F/180°C
8. Take your tarts out to rest once cooled; serve when ready

Butter Balls

The final tally has begun! Is it true that we are only a few days away? No Christmas cookie platter would be complete without Classic Swedish Butter Balls, so we're packaging them up as gifts for our neighbors.

Although Russian Tea Cakes are the more popular name for these, I prefer Butter Balls since, let's face it, that's precisely what they are. Little butter balls with sugar coating. So straightforward yet so ideal.

Preparation time: 30 Minutes
Cooking Time: 10 Minutes
Serves: 4

Ingredients

- Icing Sugar, for coating
- Vanilla Extract, 5.7g (0.16 oz)
- Pecan Extract, 5.7g (0.16 oz)
- Chopped Pecans, 128g (4.5 oz)
- Icing Sugar, 128g (4.5 oz)
- Butter, 128g (4.5 oz)
- Pastry Flour, 320g (11.2 oz)

Instructions

1. In a large bowl, add your sugar and butter
2. Beat them well until the mixture becomes light and fluffy

3. Add in the pecan, vanilla extract, and flour
4. Make a dough from the mixture
5. Form small balls and bake your balls at 350°F/175°C for 5-10 minutes
6. When the balls are finished cooking, coat the balls with icing sugar
7. Once cooled, serve when ready

Cardamom And Raspberry Buns

Cardamom, which has its roots in Indonesia and the Indian subcontinent, is commonly used in Middle Eastern and Indian cuisine. Think of the Garam Masala spice blend, rice dishes, pastries, Chai Tea, and Turkish coffee.

Cardamom has a complex flavor and is a potent perfume. It is also frequently used in Nordic cuisine, especially in Sweden, where you can discover the delectable Cardamom Bun (Kardemummabullar).

Preparation time: 30 Minutes
Cooking Time: 25 Minutes
Serves: 4

Ingredients

- Sour Cream, 16.7g (0.66 oz)
- Sugar, 64g (2.25 oz)
- Eggs, Use Three
- Active Yeast, 2.84g (0.10 oz)
- Milk, 128g (2.25 oz)
- Raspberries, 128g (2.25 oz)

- Ground Cardamom, 2.84g (0.10 oz)
- All-Purpose Flour, 512g (18 oz)

Instructions

1. Grab a large bowl, add the sugar and active yeast
2. In a separate bowl, add the dry ingredient
3. Add your dry ingredients into your active yeast mixture
4. Add the sour cream and three eggs
5. Knead the dough thoroughly, then add your raspberries
6. Make small buns and place them onto a baking tray
7. Make an egg wash
8. Brush your egg mixture on top
9. Bake your buns for 20-25 minutes at 98°F/35°C
10. Once cooled, serve when ready

Västerbotten Cheese Pie

The Västerbotten cheese pie is simple to prepare beforehand and to create. You can probably guess how it got into the hearts of the Swedes. Yes, through smörgsbord.

(A buffet or selection of open sandwiches and treats presented as hors d'oeuvres.) You can find this golden pie on buffet tables at events and holidays like Midsummer. It is essentially required for a Swedish crayfish celebration.

Preparation Time: 10 Minutes
Cooking Time: 30 Minutes
Serves: 4

Ingredients

- Butter, for greasing
- Heavy Cream, 64g (2.25 oz)
- Sugar, 64g (2.25 oz)
- Västerbotten Cheese or Mozzarella 64g (2.25 oz)
- Cream Cheese, 64g (2.25 oz)
- Pie Dough, as required
- Butter, 64g (2.25 oz)
- Golden Syrup, 28.3g (1 oz)

Instructions

1. In a large bow, add your cream and beat it properly
2. Mix the cream until frothy, then add your sugar
3. Continue beating the mixture, then add the butter
4. Beat the mixture again, adding in the Västerbotten cheese/mozzarella, cream cheese, and golden syrup
5. Continue mixing all the ingredients until they are thoroughly combined
6. Lay the pie dough into a greased pie dish
7. Add the cream cheese mixture on top
8. Bake your pie for 20-30 minutes at 350°F/180°C
9. Once cooled, serve when ready (Can be eaten hot)

Brownies

For many years, my grandparents ran a bakery in the heart of Stockholm. My mother's mother, who we refer to as "our Mormor," used to come to visit us and bake all of her delectable Swedish delicacies as we were growing up. This is one of my most favorite brownie recipes and one of our family's traditional Swedish dishes.

Preparation Time: 10 Minutes
Cooking Time: 20 Minutes
Serves: 4

Ingredients

- Kosher Salt, 2.84g (0.10 oz)
- Sugar, 16.7g (0.66 oz)
- Chopped Walnuts, 64g (2.25 oz)
- Baking Powder, 5.7g (0.16 oz)
- Cocoa Powder, 28.3g (1 oz)
- Sour cream, 128g (4.5 oz)
- Eggs, Use Three
- Unbleached White Flour, 256g (9 oz)
- Unsalted Melted Butter, 128g (4.5 oz)
- Baking Soda, 5.7g (0.16 oz)

Instructions

1. In a large bowl, add your eggs
2. Beat the eggs until they turn frothy and creamy
3. Add the melted butter and sour cream into the mixture
4. Add the sugar and beat the mixture for five minutes
5. In a separate bowl, add all the dry ingredients
6. Gently add the dry mix into your wet mix and fold your batter
7. Pour the batter into a greased dish
8. Bake your brownies for 10-20 minutes at 350°F/180°C
9. Once cooled, serve when ready

Swedish Pastry

A Danish pastry, or Wienerbrod in Danish, is a multilayered, laminated sweet pastry made in the viennoiserie tradition. The name is commonly abbreviated to just Danish (particularly in American English).

The idea was introduced to Denmark by Austrian bakers, and once the Danish people modified the recipe to their desire, it became a Danish specialty. It's a puff pastry with a layered texture composed of laminated yeast-leavened dough, much like other viennoiserie pastries, for example, croissants.

Preparation time: 20 Minutes
Cooking Time: 20 Minutes
Serves: 4

Ingredients

- Egg, Use One
- Baking Soda, a pinch
- Flour, 128g (4.5 oz)
- Ground Cardamom, 5.7g (0.16 oz)
- Sugar, 16.7g (0.66 oz)
- Butter, 64g (2.25 oz)

For The Filling

- Cinnamon, 1.42g (0.05 oz)
- Nutmeg, a pinch
- Butter, 64g (2.25 oz)
- Cream, 64g (2.25 oz)
- Sugar, 64g (2.25 oz)
- Blanched Almonds, 64g (2.25 oz)

Instructions

1. In a large bowl, make the pastry by mixing all the ingredients
2. Make the dough and cut it into square shapes and place them on a baking dish
3. Grease the baking dish properly and line the inside of the plate with parchment paper
4. Cook your almond mixture by mixing up all the ingredients
5. Add your almond mixture into the middle of your pastry and fold the pastry dough
6. Bake your pies at 350°F/180°C for 15-20 minutes
7. Once cooled, serve when ready

Kringles

Danish Kringles are a pastry similar to other Danish pastries loaded with cheese, fruits, nuts, and other ingredients. The shape of the pretzel was modified to its current oval shape in the United States (not Denmark) to eliminate the unfilled, overlapping areas. Over time, various fruit and nut fillings were also introduced.

True kringles require up to thirty layers of delicate pastry dough to make, which is a labor-intensive process that can take three days. Rolling butter thinly between multiple layers of yeast-raised dough presents a difficulty for kringle bakers.

Preparation time: 20 Minutes
Cooking Time: 20 Minutes
Serves:4

Ingredients

- Almond Extract, 2.84g (0.10 oz)
- White Sugar, 64g (2.25 oz) for spreading on top
- Large Eggs, Use Two
- Salted Butter, 128g (4.5 oz)
- White Sugar, 64g (2.25 oz)
- Heavy Cream, 14.3g (0.50 oz)
- Flour, 448g (15.8 oz)
- Vanilla Extract, 5.7g (0.16 oz)

Instructions

1. Grab a large bowl, and make the pastry dough by mixing all the ingredients
2. Cut the dough into square shapes and place them onto a greased baking dish with parchment paper
3. Bake your pastries at 350°F/180°C for 15-20 minutes
4. For the icing, add the almond extract, sugar, and cream into a small bowl
5. Beat it well
6. When the pastry is baked, dish it out
7. Spread the formed icing on top and serve when ready

Butter Cookies

Danish biscuits, also known as butter cookies or butter biscuits, are cookies made with butter, flour, and sugar that have their origins in Denmark. They are Danish cookies that resemble shortbread cookies.

Due to its texture, partly due to the quantity of butter and sugar used, the butter cookie is often referred to as a "crisp cookie." your dough should often chill to allow for good handling and manipulation.

Preparation Time: 20 Minutes
Cooking Time: 20 Minutes
Serves: 4

Ingredients

- Kosher Salt, 2.84g (0.10 oz)
- Sliced Almonds, 16.7g (0.66 oz)
- Large Eggs, Use Two
- Almond Extract, 14.3g (0.50 oz)
- Salted Butter, 128g (4.5 oz)
- White Sugar, 128g (4.5 oz)
- Flour, 448g (15.8 oz)

Instructions

1. Take out a large bowl
2. Add the dry ingredients into the bowl
3. Mix all the ingredients well

4. Add the butter to the wet ingredients
5. Add the eggs and sliced almonds into the cookie mixture
6. Add the formed mixture into a piping bag
7. Make small round cookies on a greased baking dish
8. Bake your cookies at 350°F/180°C for 15-20 minutes
9. Once cooled down, serve when ready

Cake Doughnuts

Cake donuts from Norway include smultring (plural: smultringer) and hjortetakk (often spelled hjorte bakkels). They are often made without a glaze or filling and are frequently spiced with cardamom, cinnamon, lemon, orange zest, and different liqueurs.

Preparation Time: 10 Minutes
Cooking Time: 5 Minutes
Serves: 4

Ingredients

- Baking Soda, 5.7g (0.16 oz)
- Cardamom Sugar, to taste
- Cognac, 28.3g (1 oz)
- Whipped Cream, 64g (2.25 oz)
- Flour, 1024g (36 oz)
- Sugar, 256g (9 oz)
- Eggs, Use Eight
- Butter, 64g (2.25 oz)

Instructions

1. Grab a large bowl, mix all your ingredients well
2. Form a semi-thick batter from the mixture
3. Heat a pan full of oil
4. Make doughnut-like cake structures with the help of a piping bag
5. Fry your doughnut cakes at 375°F190°C
6. Let your doughnuts cool down
7. Add the cinnamon sugar on top (Optional)
8. Serve when ready

Krumkake

The Norwegian waffle cookie, known as krumkake, is made of flour, butter, eggs, sugar, and cream. Krumkake is Norwegian for "curved cake" and is available in the plural as krumkake.

The thin round cakes, resembling the Sicilian cannoli and Italian pizzelle, are typically baked on a distinctive ornate two-sided iron griddle.

Modern electric iron griddles offer the ease of nonstick surfaces, automatic timing, and numerous cakes per batch, in contrast to older iron griddles used over the stove. The 13–20 cm (5-8 inch) krumkake is rolled into little cones while still hot and placed in a wooden or plastic cone.

Krumkake can be consumed simply or stuffed with ingredients like whipped cream (typically multekrem).

Preparation Time: 10 minutes
Cooking Time: 5 Minutes
Serves: 4

Note: Two-sided iron griddle required

Ingredients

- Vanilla Extract, 2.84g (0.10 oz)
- Eggs, Use Two
- All-Purpose Flour, 192g (6.7 0z)
- White Sugar, 128g (4.5 oz)
- Butter Flavoring, 2.84g (0.10 oz)
- Unsalted Butter, 64g (2.25 oz)
- Milk, 128g (4.5 oz)

Instructions

1. In a large bowl, add the eggs
2. Beat the eggs until they become creamy and fluffy
3. Add in the white sugar and mix
4. Combine the remaining ingredients and mix thoroughly
5. Preheat an iron
6. Add a tablespoon, 1.42g (0.05oz) of the mixture onto the iron and cook on both sides
7. Once cooked, roll it immediately before it hardens
8. Serve when ready

Julekake

Norwegian Christmas cake is known as Jule Kake. It is an almond, raisin, and candied fruit-filled yeast cake that is baked with butter, sugar, and cardamom. Instead of cake, it is sometimes referred to as "Christmas bread." Either warm or toasted with butter.

Preparation Time:30 Minutes
Cooking Time: 20 Minutes
Serves: 4

Ingredients

- Egg Wash, as required
- Scalded Milk, 256g (9 oz)
- Active Yeast, two packets
- All-Purpose Flour, 768g (27 oz)
- Orange Zest, 5.7g (0.16 oz)
- Cinnamon Powder, 5.7g (0.16 oz)
- Dry Fruits, 256g (9.0 oz)
- Sugar, 64g (2.25 oz)
- Butter, 128g (4.5 oz)
- Eggs, Use Two
- Cardamom Seeds, 1.42g (0.05 oz)

Instructions

1. Grab a large bowl, add all the dry ingredients, and mix
2. In a separate bowl, add the two eggs and beat them
3. Add the other wet ingredients into the mixture

4. Pour the dry ingredients into the wet mixture
5. Knead the dough with light hands
6. Add the dough to a greased baking dish
7. Apply the egg wash on top of the bread
8. Bake the bread at 350°F/180°C for 15-20 minutes
9. Once cooled, cut and serve when ready

Pecan Cookies

These Pecan Cookies are pretty famous in Sweden! Shortbread dough rich in butter and brown sugar is tucked under a pecan half. They go well with milk or coffee, perhaps even tea, and are ideal for cookie plates.

Preparation Time: 20 Minutes
Cooking Time: 20 Minutes
Serves: 4

Ingredients

- Kosher Salt, 2.84g (0.10 oz)
- Large Eggs, Two
- Chopped Pecans, 64g (2.25 oz)
- Salted Butter, 128g (4.5 oz)
- White Sugar, 64g (2.25 oz)
- Flour, 448g (15.8 oz)
- Vanilla Extract, 5.7g (0.16 oz)

Instructions

1. Take out a large bowl
2. Combine all the dry ingredients into the bowl
3. Mix all the dry ingredients well
4. Add the butter to the wet ingredients using a separate bowl
5. Add the yeast mixture and eggs into the cookie mixture
6. Add a spoon full of 14.3g (0.50 oz) of the mixture onto a baking dish
7. Add the chopped pecans on top and bake your cookies at 350°F/180°C for 15-20 minutes
8. Once cooled, serve when ready

Butter Buns

The so-called "bollos de mantequilla" is a relatively short pastry. They are a brioche or Swiss bun split in half and filled with butter and egg cream. They frequently have sugar sprinkled on top. They are inexplicably soft to the touch and reasonably delicious. They were said to have originated in 1813.

Preparation Time: 30 Minutes
Cooking Time: 25 Minutes
Serves: 4

Ingredients

- Egg Wash, as required
- Butter, 16.7g (0.66 oz)
- Sugar, 64g (2.25 oz)
- Eggs, Use Three

- Active Yeast, 2.84g (0.10 oz)
- Milk, 128g (4.5 oz)
- Ground Cardamom, 2.84g (0.10 oz)

Instructions

1. Grab a large bowl, add the sugar and active yeast
2. In a separate bowl, add the dry ingredients
3. Add your active yeast mixture into your dry ingredients
4. Add the eggs and butter
5. Knead your dough
6. Make small buns and place them onto a greased baking tray
7. Brush the egg wash on top
8. Bake your buns for 15-20 minutes at 350°F/180°C
9. Once cooled, serve when ready

Apple Tart

A Dutch-style 'Appeltaart' pastry is typically made with butter, sugar, flour, egg, and baking powder. The dough is exceptionally soft in that it is carefully pressed by hand into form after being chilled.

The way the ingredients rise and envelope the fresh apple filling makes this dish unique. What defines the 'appeltaart' is the number of apples used to bake it — when baked well — it looks like a mountain of apples just barely held together by a buttery crust.

Preparation Time: 10 Minutes
Cooking Time: 30 Minutes
Serves: 4

Ingredients

- Butter, for greasing
- Sliced Apples, 64g (2.25 oz)
- Sugar, 64g (2.25 oz)
- Cream, 64g (2.25 oz)
- Tart Dough, as required
- Butter, 64g (2.25 oz)
- Golden Syrup, 28.3g (1 oz)

Instructions

1. In a large bowl, add your cream and beat it properly
2. Make it creamy and frothy, then add the sugar
3. Continue beating the mixture and add the butter
4. Continue beating your mixture, adding the sliced apples and golden syrup
5. Continue mixing until all your ingredients are well combined
6. Lay the tart dough into greased tart dishes
7. Add the apple mixture on top
8. Bake your tarts at 350°F/180°C for 25-30 minutes
9. Once cooled, serve when ready

Cardamom Cake

Most Swedes would list cardamom cake among their top ten favorite traditional Fika foods. Kardemummakaka is typically eaten simply with a strong cup of coffee, but on occasion, it is served with a little whipped cream and some fresh fruit. You can make it in a round or an oblong tin.

Preparation Time: 10 Minutes
Cooking Time: 20 Minutes
Serves:4

Ingredients

- Kosher Salt, 2.84g (0.10 oz)
- Sugar, 128g (4.5 oz)
- Ground Cinnamon, 5.7g (0.16 oz)
- Freshly Ground Cardamom, 8.4g (0.33 oz)
- Eggs, Use Three
- Unbleached White Flour, 256g (9 oz)
- Unsalted Melted Butter, 128g (4.5 oz)
- Baking Soda, 5.7g (0.16 oz)

Instructions

1. In a large bowl, add the eggs
2. Beat eggs until they become frothy and creamy
3. Add the melted butter into the mixture
4. Add the sugar and beat the mixture for five more minutes
5. In another bowl, add the dry ingredients

6. Gently add the dry mix into your wet mix and fold your batter
7. Pour the batter into a greased baking tray
8. Bake the cake for 20-15 minutes at 350°F/180°C
9. Once cooled, serve when ready

Rhubarb

Rhubarb grows well in the relaxed environment of Norway, where this delightful breakfast cake is from. Rhubarb is a well-liked ingredient wherever it succeeds because it is perennial, abundant, and one of the first crops of spring.

(It grows throughout the northern part of the United States, but for the rest of you, it's in the produce section.) This time of year, rhubarb's tart, berry-like flavor pairs beautifully with almonds to create an incredibly delicious coffee cake.

Preparation Time: 10 Minutes
Cooking Time: 20 Minutes
Serves: 4

Ingredients

- Sour Cream, 64g (2.25 oz)
- Kosher Salt, 2.84 (0.10 oz)
- Sugar, 16.7g (0.66 oz)
- Chopped Almonds, 2.84 (0.10 oz)
- Baking Powder, 5.7g (0.10 oz)
- Chopped Rhubarb, 128g (4.5 oz)
- Eggs, Use Three

- Unbleached White Flour, 256g (9 oz)
- Unsalted Melted Butter, 128g (4.5 oz)
- Baking Soda, 5.7g (0.16 oz)

Instructions

1. In a large bowl, add the eggs
2. Beat eggs until they become frothy and creamy
3. Add the sour cream and butter into the mixture
4. Add the sugar and continue beating the mixture for five more minutes
5. In a separate bowl, add the dry ingredients
6. gently add the dry mix into your wet mix and fold your batter
7. Pour your batter into a greased baking dish
8. Add the chopped rhubarb and almonds in the end and bake your cake at 350°F/180°C for 15-20 minutes
9. Once cooled, serve when ready

Dream Cake

This Danish Dream Cake, also known as "Drmmekage fra Brovst," is from the Jutland village of Brovst. This cake has been a favorite of Danes ever since a young girl entered a competition using her grandmother's unpublished family recipe and won. It makes sense, given that the cake is surprisingly light, fluffy, and has a delectable coconut topping.

Preparation Time: 10 Minutes
Cooking Time: 20 Minutes
Serves: 4

Ingredients

- Kosher Salt, 2.84g (0.10 oz)
- Sugar, 128g (4.5 oz)
- Eggs, Use Three
- Unbleached White Flour, 256g (9 oz)
- Unsalted Melted Butter, 128g (4.5 oz)
- Baking Soda, 5.7g (0.16 oz)

For The Topping

- Brown Sugar, 28.3g (1 oz)
- Milk, 64g (2.25 oz)
- Coconut Flakes, 64g 92.25 oz)
- Butter, 28.3g (1 oz)

Instructions

1. In a large bowl, add the eggs
2. Beat eggs until they become frothy and creamy
3. Add the melted butter into the mixture
4. Add the sugar and beat the mixture for five more minutes
5. Grab a separate bowl, add your dry ingredients
6. Slowly add your dry ingredients into your wet mix and fold your batter
7. Pour your mix into a greased baking dish
8. In a separate bowl, add your topping mixture and beat it thoroughly
9. Pour your topping mixture on top of your cake batter
10. Bake your cake for 15-20 minutes at, 350°F/180°C
11. Once cooled, serve when ready

Kransekake

The national cake of Scandinavia, known as "Kransekake," also known as "Wreath Cake" or "Ring Cake," has earned a prestigious place on wedding, birthday, graduation, and holiday banquet tables. A typical Kransekake should contain at least 18 rings, although more festive cakes might have many more layers.

These rings are generally stacked on top of one another and secured with icing. This cake is a favorite among both Danes and Norwegians. During the Christmas season, it is simple to find and purchase kransekake.

Preparation Time: 10 Minutes
Cooking Time: 20 Minutes
Serves: 4

Note: *This recipe requires Kransekake molds.*

Ingredients

- Unsalted Butter for greasing
- Icing Sugar, 384g (13.5 oz)
- Egg Whites, Use Two
- Sliced Almonds, 64g (2.25 oz)

For The Topping

- Brown Sugar, 128g 92.25 oz)
- A drop of your choice of food coloring
- Egg Whites, Use Three

Instructions

1. In a large bowl, add egg whites
2. Add the melted butter into the mixture
3. Beat eggs until they become frothy and creamy
4. Add the sugar and crushed almonds
5. Beat the mixture for five more minutes
6. Add your batter into the kransekake molds
7. In a separate bowl, add the topping mixture and beat well
8. Bake your kransekake for 15-20 minutes at, 350°F/180°C
9. Once cooled, add you're formed topping on top
10. Serve when ready

Pancake Puffs

Aebleskivers or pancake puffs are a type of pancake cooked in semi-circular molds with a nearly creamy middle and a crisp, caramelized rim. Although that could perhaps conjure up an image of an undercooked pancake, be assured that an aebleskiver is nothing like that.

Although you might find them as part of a European breakfast, here in the dish's original country, we serve them for afternoon coffee breaks or on cold winter nights. They are generally served in groups of three.

Preparation Time: 10 Minutes
Cooking Time: 20 Minutes
Serves: 4

Note: *Aebleskivers maker, required.*

Ingredients

- Milk, 192g (6.7 oz)
- Blackberries, as desired
- Sliced Bananas, as desired
- Flour, 192g (6.7 oz)
- Maple Syrup, 1.42g (0.05 oz)
- Butter, 16.7g (0.66 oz)
- Sugar, 85.8g (3 oz)
- Sliced Strawberries, as required
- Egg Whites, Use Three

Instructions

1. In a large bowl, add the eggs whites
2. Beat the egg whites until they become frothy and creamy
3. Add the melted butter into the mixture
4. Add the sugar and crushed almonds
5. Beat the mixture for five more minutes
6. Add in the remaining ingredients and fold your batter
7. Bake your puffy pancakes for 15-20 minutes (Aebleskivers maker, required)
8. Once cooled, serve when ready

Cinnamon Rolls

Sweet rolls have been around since ancient times. However, the arrival of cinnamon spice to Europe resulted in the creation of this unique sweet treat. The cinnamon rolls we know today are thought to have originated in Sweden. They are called *kanelbulle* and are celebrated on October 4th as a national holiday. You can easily enjoy these rolls with a hot beverage of your choice.

Preparation time: 30 Minutes
Cooking Time: 25 Minutes
Serves: 4

Ingredients

- White Sugar, 16.7g (0.66 oz)
- Eggs, Use Three
- Milk. 128g (4.5 oz)
- Butter, 64g (2.25 oz)
- Brown Sugar, 64g 92.25 oz)
- Ground Cinnamon, 2.84g (0.10 oz)
- All-Purpose Flour,512g (36 oz)

Instructions

1. Grab a large bowl, and add to it the sugar and active yeast.
2. In a separate bowl, add the dry ingredients.
3. Add the active yeast mixture to the dry ingredients.
4. Add the eggs and butter.
5. Knead your dough thoroughly.
6. In a small bowl, add the cinnamon powder and sugar.
7. Roll your dough and add the cinnamon mixture and brown sugar on top
8. Roll to form a log structure
9. Cut slices and add pearl sugar on top in a greased baking dish.
10. Bake your cinnamon rolls for 20-25 minutes at, 350°F/180°C
11. Once cooled, serve when ready.

Happy Baking! Glad Baking!

Printed in Great Britain
by Amazon

12083414R00027